IMAGES OF ENGLAND

TORQUAY
A CENTURY OF CHANGE

Torquay from Stantiford Hill

IMAGES OF ENGLAND

TORQUAY
A CENTURY OF CHANGE

ALAN HEATHER AND DAVID MASON

Alan S. Heather.

TEMPUS

First published 2006

Tempus Publishing Limited
The Mill, Brimscombe Port,
Stroud, Gloucestershire, GL5 2QG
www.tempus-publishing.com

British Library Cataloguing in Publication Data.
A catalogue record for this book is available from the British Library.

ISBN 0 7524 3960 X

Typesetting and origination by Tempus Publishing Limited.
Printed in Great Britain.

Contents

Torquay from Park Hill.

Introduction

When David Mason and I were first invited to compile this book we were both delighted. We spent many happy hours researching further into our local heritage and presenting the results in a format which will be at the same time entertaining and a useful reference. It could not have been done without access to David's vast collection of postcards and some early photographs by Francis Bedford which to the best of our knowledge have never been published in a book before. My input as a former journalist was the text, so it was a team effort which we both enjoyed.

This is not intended purely as a history book. It is a book of images taken through many decades, although when you read the text it will inevitably encourage you to delve further into the history of the town. The importance of photographic images as a valuable archive of past times cannot be exaggerated. We are proud to have been given the opportunity to add to that archive in this volume.

The Napoleonic wars meant that the rich elite, unable to travel on the continent, looked for pleasant places to visit here at home. So it was that the small fishing village of Torquay, which only had a population of 838 in 1801, swiftly grew to 11,474 by 1851. The nobility and gentry, who led a lifestyle which demanded the employment of many servants, chose to reside or spend the winter season in the town, attracted by the lovely scenery and an equable climate. Many fine villas were erected on the south-facing terraces of the town to accommodate them. New hotels were built and older establishments were enlarged and improved to meet the needs of the high class clientele, particularly after the arrival of the railway to Torquay.

Great emphasis was made on the equability of Torquay's climate. So Torquay developed as a 'watering place' and was known as a place where you could benefit from the 'salubrious airs'. The possible advantages of consumptive invalids benefiting from a stay in the town was clearly recognised and promoted. Catering for the sick became a real money spinner in an environment guaranteed to soothe.

To support the lifestyle of the nobility and gentry shopkeepers and other service industries were eager to cater for every request and whim. Demand soon grew for souvenirs and other mementoes for the visitor to take home as a reminder of a pleasant stay in the area. Very popular were books of etchings, lithographs and aquatints which offered artistic depictions of the town and environments. By the middle of the nineteenth century publishers like Rock and Besley were producing booklets of twelve or twenty-four engravings selling within the range of 1s [5p] to 2s 6d [12.5p].

All this was to change with the arrival of affordable photography in the late 1850s, and local photographers like William Widger of Torquay and William Spreat of Exeter were soon offering *carte de visite* and stereograph images of the town to purchase as souvenirs. Spreat was a former artist and lithographer who produced many fine lithographs of the town in previous decades but saw in the new medium of photography a fresh way of satisfying his artistic talents. Within a few years the demand for artist-drawn souvenirs had quickly evaporated and photographic images were in demand.

In 1863, Francis Bedford came to Torquay on the first of several visits. He was considered one of England's more significant landscape photographers. Bedford was born in 1816 into the middle-class family of Francis Octavius Bedford, a London architect of some distinction. Francis junior trained as an architect and was also a skilled lithographer. He turned to photography in the early 1850s, and was one of the founder members of the Photographic Society in 1853. His first landscape work was of north Wales, which appeared in a book published in 1855. In 1857 he received a commission from Queen Victoria to photograph views of Coburg, as a gift for Prince Albert. Another commission followed in 1862, when he accompanied HRH the Prince of Wales to record his tour of the Middle East. During the two decades that Bedford visited Torquay the population grew by fifty per cent at a time of rapid development for Torquay. We have dedicated chapter two of this book to a selection of his fine images, many captured through his lens over 140 years ago.

These were pioneering times and photography continued to excite and attract the attention of Victorians for several decades. The next leap forward was the introduction of postcards to Great Britain in 1894. The early cards were printed and it was not until 1902 that the first photographic postcards started to appear. This was a time of great popularity for the postcard, which was a cheap and dependable way of communicating with friends and family in the days when the telephone was only used in business and in the homes of the wealthy. The photographic postcard opened up a brand new market both for national and local photographers to issue local view cards, and also feature personalities, events, charabanc outings, sports and a whole new range of uses which photographers were quick to exploit. Thank goodness they did, for their legacy is the tremendous range of social history material which receives pride of place in any topographical postcard collection.

In this book we therefore pay tribute to the artists of the early nineteenth century and the photographers who followed. It is a valuable archive they have left which has allowed us to compile this book for your interest and enjoyment.

It is important that our heritage in Torquay is not forgotten and allowed to disappear.

Alan Heather
May 2006

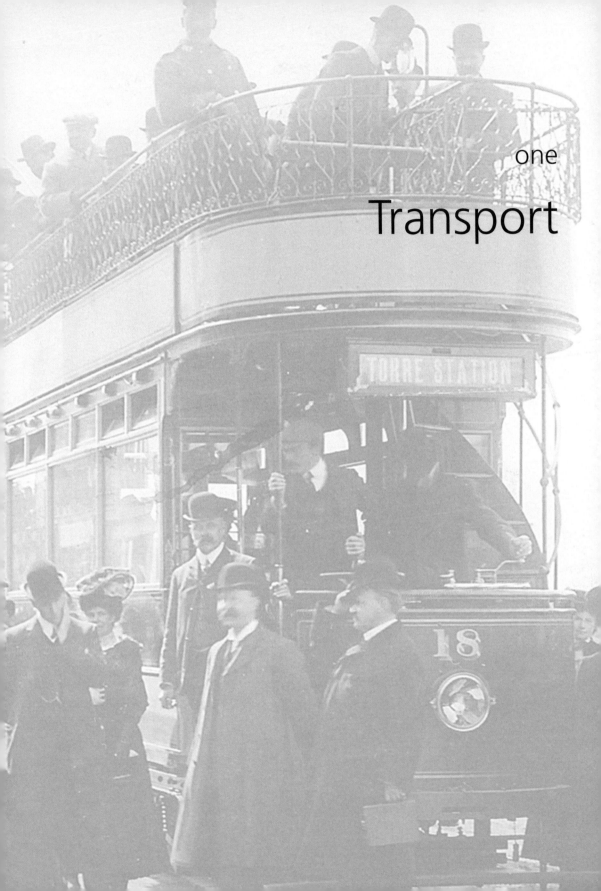

one

Transport

Torquay as a town only has a short history but one building has great antiquity: Torre Abbey, which was founded by six canons of the Premonstratensian Order in 1196. In 1539, with the dissolution of the monasteries it became a ruin. The medieval cloister was virtually unscathed and in 1598 was converted into a house by Thomas Ridgeway. After a succession of various owners it was bought in 1662 by the Cary family and was for over 250 years their home. In 1930 it was sold to Torquay Borough Council.

Opposite above: This map from around 1840 shows the road system at a time when all travel to and from Torquay would have been by road or sea. Carriers traded from Torquay and other main towns in south Devon, carrying goods to other areas on a daily or weekly basis.

Opposite below: This advertisement appeared in 1837 and mentions Queen Victoria's Coronation. A connecting horse driven carriage to Exeter provided the south Devon traveller with the means to reach London in about twenty-four hours. The other method of travel to London was by the *Brunswick*, a steam coastal vessel, for those who preferred a sea voyage.

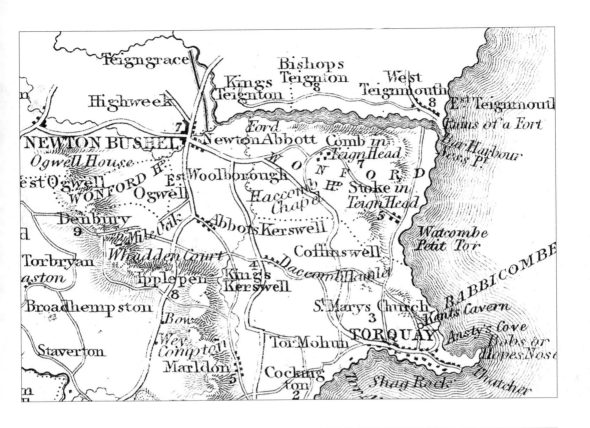

Steam trains first reached Torre Station in December 1848, affording people a quicker means of travel to Bristol, London and beyond. They were so successful it was decided that the South Devon Railway Company should extend the line to Torquay, Paignton and eventually to Kingswear. In January 1858 Sir Lawrence Palk, MP for south Devon, cut the first sod in a field near Torre station amid great celebrations. He is portrayed here depositing it into a ceremonial 'tip'.

Right: The ceremonial wheelbarrow and spade used by Sir Lawrence were manufactured by Ash and Son, coachbuilders, at their works at Union Street, Torquay. These workmen are proudly displaying the implements.

Below: This photograph from around 1910, taken some fifty years after the railway was extended to Paignton, shows a steam passenger train passing near the Livermead House Hotel.

From the 1890s to the 1930s the paddle steamer *Duchess of Devonshire* became a familiar sight along the south Devon coast, offering half-day and full-day excursions, which were a popular attraction to both holiday makers and residents.

Above: The Duchess is seen here during the first decade of the 1900s disembarking and embarking passengers at Oddicombe Beach, Torquay. In 1934 the vessel was grounded at Sidmouth. Attempts to re-float her proved unsuccessful and the vessel was eventually broken up on the beach.

Opposite above: In 1905 there were few buses in Torquay and the tram service would not begin until 1907. The gentry, however, were well served by horse cabs which operated from ranks in the town and also popular residential areas. This rank was situated opposite St Matthias' church at Wellswood.

Below: Bernard and 'Kitty' were regularly stationed by Cary Parade opposite the Torbay Hotel. They were popular characters for many years with visitors and residents and very willing to take them to places of local interest.

Within a few years horsepower would be replaced within the furniture removal and cartage business by steam wagons, and eventually motor-driven pantechnicons would become the normal method of transport. Here is a very well-laden wagon belonging to H.J. Blunt of Ellacombe.

By the 1860s most of the leading Torquay hotels had their own horse-drawn buses to collect patrons from the railway station. This vehicle from around 1905 belonged to the Victoria and Albert Hotel in Belgrave Road.

In July 1904 the Great Western Railway Company introduced a Motor Omnibus feeder service linking its railway station in Paignton with the GWR office in Vaughan Parade. Two vehicles were used, a single-decker and an open topped double-decker. It was petrol driven, had solid tyres and held eighteen passengers inside and twenty on the top deck. The photograph was taken on its first day of service while it halted outside the Torbay Hotel. The 4d single fare proved popular.

In 1905 work began by the Torquay Tramway Company to provide a tram service to Torre Station, Beacon Quay, St Marychurch and Babbacombe, Wellswood and Ellacombe. The work involved great disruption in the town with the laying of the track. This is the scene in the Strand.

Fifteen months after the start of track laying the service was officially opened on 4 April 1907 when the first tram car left Beacon Quay for Torre Station. Instead of operating by the normal overhead line the operators chose the Dolter system, whereby the tram activated a stud placed between the tracks at intervals to drive the vehicle forward.

The Dolter system proved unreliable and in 1911 the decision was taken to convert the complete service to overhead supply lines. This involved 448 poles and fifteen miles of copper wire. The work was completed on 6 March 1911 and included the extension of the service to Paignton. This picture was taken at least fifteen years later on the Strand and clearly shows the overhead lines.

The tramway service closed in 1934 and was replaced by motor omnibuses. The possibility of replacing the trams with a trolley bus service had been discussed but came to nothing. This tram in the early 1920s is in a very quiet Victoria Parade.

The King's Yacht entering Tor Bay, July 1910.

In July 1910 it had been arranged that HM King George V and Queen Mary would board the royal yacht to inspect the combined fleets at Mount's Bay. Bad weather off Cornwall forced the review of the combined fleet to be rescheduled to Tor Bay. There were over 200 vessels, including thirty-seven battleships and twenty-seven cruisers, and the review took place over two days.

MR GRAHAM WHITE READY TO FLY OVER THE FLEET IN TORBAY

Pioneering aviator Claude Graham White brought his Firman biplane to Torquay for the occasion, affording many people their first opportunity to see a flying machine. It was only seven years after the Wright brothers had established that man-made flight was possible.

On 27 July he made two flights from Torre Abbey Meadow over the assembled might of the British navy and their majesties aboard the royal yacht.

The overhead flights bought to the attention of the Lords of the Admiralty the vulnerability of shipping to air attack and also the need to alter the elevation of the guns to cope with this new and threatening means of warfare.

The early motor charabancs were limited to 12mph and had solid tyres which limited the distance they could travel. This Torquay Co-op staff outing would have been an eagerly awaited annual event.

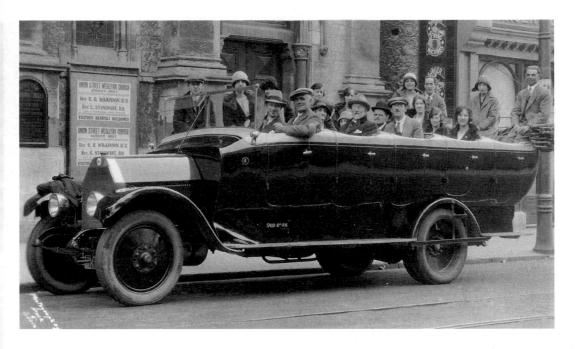

Above: By the 1930s the speed and comfort of travel by charabanc had improved. This is a choir outing from Union Street Methodist church.

Below: In the earlier years of the 1900s family and private traders predominated over the national firms now common in every High Street. Such a family firm was Callard's the bakers, who successfully traded for several generations in Torquay. Mr Callard here proudly presents his first motor-driven delivery van, *c.* 1918.

DAILY AT THE CLOCK TOWER, STRAND.

FREE MOTOR SERVICE TO AND FROM
THE HOTEL AT FREQUENT INTERVALS.

Left: During the 1920s and 1930s a few of the leading Torquay hotels still retained motor buses to collect and return their patrons to the railway station or to take them on trips. This vehicle belongs to the Torquay Hydro Hotel by Daddy Hole Plain, which was a popular hotel at the time. It is parked by the Mallock Clock Tower.

Below: Although this motor omnibus does not display a company livery it does indicate that by the 1920s the routes were becoming longer and not just confined to a one town operation. This service covered Torquay, Newton Abbot and Ashburton.

TORQUAY-NEWTON-ASHBURTON

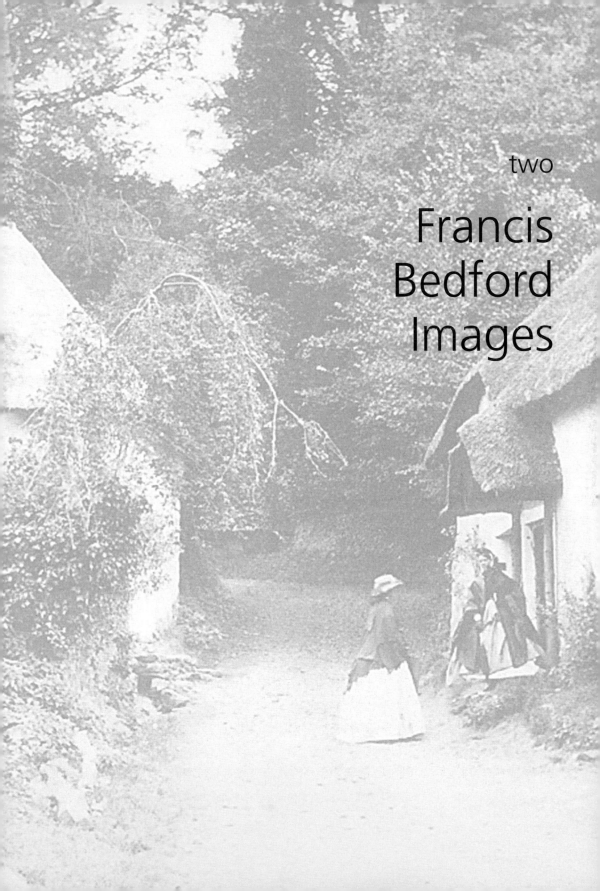

two

Francis Bedford Images

Outside the front of Cockington Court stand Charles Herbert Mallock, his wife Maria and six of his daughters. Born in 1802 he inherited the estate in 1846 and died in 1873. He had a total of seven daughters and three sons. The girls have been playing croquet.

Opposite above: Cockington Court. This Georgian mansion was for several generations the home of the Mallock family. It still retains part of the old house, which dates back many centuries.

Opposite below: Cockington Forge and Home Farm. Although the buildings in view have been adapted over the years this scene is instantly recognisable. The ladies' costume dates this photograph to the 1860s.

Above: This picture Bedford captioned 'Farm Yard at Chelston'. The farm was demolished long ago to make way for Torquay's ever-increasing population.

Right: Livermead Cottage was said to have been erected in 1825. At the time of this image by Bedford in the early 1860s it was a lodging house. It was gutted by fire in January 1886. The Livermead Cliff Hotel now occupies the site.

Opposite above: This is Cockington church, parts of which date from the 1200s. Bedford took a long time to set up his exposures. The lighting together with lack of movement from trees and vegetation was important. He would sometimes tie down branches to stop movement spoiling the exposure.

Oppposite below: Court Cottage, also called Court House, was later the local school during the early 1900s.

Above: Torbay Road or Station Road, as it was known some two decades after it was built, is still a rough unmade road in this picture. The lane to the left leads to the recently opened railway station. In the middle distance is a toll house opposite where King's Drive now joins Torquay Road.

St Luke's church, consecrated in 1862 by the Bishop of Jamaica. Bedford has set up his camera in Croft Road. Nearby his coachman patiently waits before taking him to the next point of interest.

Opposite below: Atkinson's Family Hotel, later the Belgrave Hotel, which was opened in 1862. It was one of several fine new hotels erected during the decade.

Cash's Family Hotel, later the Victoria and Albert Hotel and now the Victoria Hotel, opened in 1867. It had two entrances so that carriages could call at front door and leave by the second entrance or exit.

St Saviour's, the parish church of Torre or Tormohun, has parts of the building dating back to Norman times. This photograph from the early 1860s was only a decade or so after the restoration of 1849-50.

From Waldon Hill we look back over the higher parts of the town towards Upton. In the foreground can be seen Warren Road, Cotswold, and the line of Abbey Road.

On the left is St John's Chapel of Ease, and adjacent the new St John's church is emerging. In the middle distance can be seen Higher Terrace, and beyond Lisburne Crescent and the Lincombes.

Looking down from Waldon Hill can be seen Cary Green together with the beach, which within a few years was covered over to form a widening of the promenade in front of the newly erected Torbay Hotel, which was completed in 1867. On Cary Green can be seen a captured Russian gun from the Crimean War given to the town by the War Office. Within a year objections were raised that offence may be caused to members of the Russian royal family staying in the town at that time. It was first removed to the market then to Ellacombe Green and was not returned to Cary Green until 1874. It stayed there until the Princess Gardens were laid.

Right: Abbey Crescent was built by John Harvey and Richard Henley. It was a fine Victorian terrace later spoilt by development in the 1900s. Here it is shown in its original state just a few years after completion.

Below: A fine panorama of the harbour and Waldon Hill beyond.

Activity on the quayside as a sailing vessel is unloaded. To the left of the quay can be seen the beach at the foot of Cary Green.

Six sailing vessels are moored against the quay. During the 1800s and into the 1900s coal, timber, sand and other raw materials arrived by boat.

The Bath House, first mentioned in 1817, where Elizabeth Barrett stayed to recuperate from illness in 1838. Later in the 1800s it was demolished to make way for Sea Lawn, now the Hotel Regina. To the right can be seen Shaw's boat building yard.

The newly erected Imperial Hotel which opened in November 1866. Beyond is Beacon Hill before it was cut away to help build Haldon Pier. Nestled to the seaward side of the hill is the original Bath Saloon, the erection of which was started by the Harvey Brothers in 1853.

Hesketh Crescent, built by the Harvey Brothers, began in 1846 and remains the finest example of the many fine buildings that they erected in Torquay.

The Ilsham Valley, looking down through the playing fields towards Walls Hill. On the hill stands Stoodley Knowle, which during the 1900s became a private school run by the Sisters of Les Filles de la Croix.

Right: This is the south entrance of Kents Cavern which was in use from 1859 following publication of Darwin's *Origins of the Species*, which resulted in much interest being shown in primitive man and cave exploration. Mr J.W. Underhay, whose name appears on the notice board, was the guide for many years.

Below: Babbacombe Bay and the Gasking's Cary Arms Inn. It was and still is a popular spot to relax and enjoy the magnificent scenery.

The Giant Rock, Watcombe, was a splendid place for a picnic in Victorian and Edwardian times before the trees and vegetation were allowed to grow and obscure the majestic beauty of the surroundings. Note the horseshoe bend drive to help horse-drawn carriages to arrive and depart easily.

The Cricket Ground at Chapel Hill Cross, now Barton Road. It was officially opened on 2 August 1852. This thatched pavilion must date from the early days of the cricket club but was destroyed by a fire in 1906.

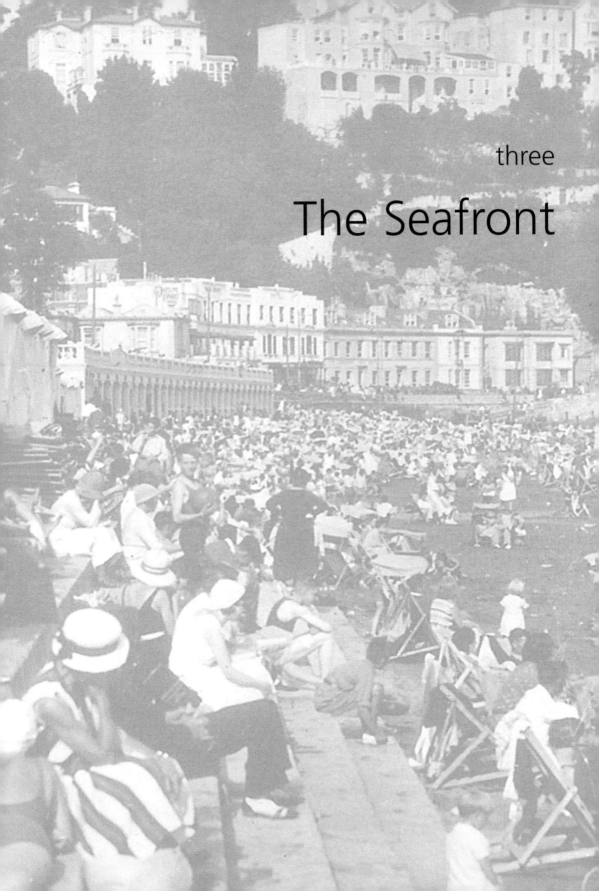

three

The Seafront

The tramway service was extended to Paignton in July 1911. The Grand Hotel opened in 1908, replacing the former structure which had originally been called the Great Western Hotel.

Passengers can be seen entering the Paignton-bound tram. This involved walking several feet into the road to meet the vehicle. Prominent is the 'big tree', which was for many years a much loved feature on the seafront until it was felled in the years between the two world wars.

Corbyn Beach, which rests below Corbyns Head, had been known variously as Cockington Beach or Chelston Beach. Corbyns Head was laid out as a recreation ground in 1886 and in 1906 was presented to the Torquay Corporation by the Mallock Estate. The tea hut was called the Corbyn Cabin.

Bathing cabins on wheels were in use on most of the Torquay beaches from Victorian times. In the early years of the last century they were replaced by bathing tents.

In a gale on 26 October 1916 the Brixham trawler *Girl Edith* was driven onto the rocks at Corbyn Head. Two of the three crew including Samuel Arnold the skipper lost their lives. Gallant attempts from the shore were made to save the boat. The Torquay lifeboat could not be launched so a Brixham boat came across and tried to use a smaller rescue boat but two lifeboat crew members lost their lives in the attempt.

The next day attempts are made to salvage the boat.

ABBEY SANDS, TORQUAY. 77

Above: Bathing tents behind Abbey Sands with the beach inspector who collected hire money from the bathers.

Below: Bathing costumes of the 1920s were less revealing than in later decades. They gave better freedom of movement than the heavy garments worn by swimmers in Victorian times.

The Colonnade was erected on Abbey Sands during the late 1920s. It contained a café and laid tables can clearly be seen between the columns.

Abbey Sands Cafe, Torquay   206542 J.V.

The café under the Colonnade used a waitress service and was a popular rendezvous for afternoon tea or morning coffee. During the height of the season the café was open until midnight.

King's Gardens were laid out and officially opened on 19 April 1904. The area contained two lakes fed by a spring rising in Sherwell Valley. A rustic bridge was built to divide the two lakes.

The larger of the two lakes in King's Gardens was designed to be used by lads of all ages to sail their model boats.

Gardener's Cottage, Torbay Road, Torquay.

Above: A young girl pauses whilst playing with her hoop in the Royal Terrace Gardens to admire the flowering aloe, a succulent tropical plant with very tall stems.

Opposite above: The toll house near Abbey Crescent when still in use for collecting tolls during the 1860s. The tolls ranged from 6d for any trap or carriage with not more than three wheels to 1s per beast drawing any heavy vehicle. The leading hotels paid money to the Torquay Turnpike Trust to save their visitors vexatious restriction.

Oppposite below: When the Royal Terrace Gardens, also known as Terrace Gardens, were laid out in 1893 the old toll house became the gardener's cottage and was sometimes called Dyers Cottage, after the gardener who was working there at that time.

Left: Near the entrance to the Princess Pier was a drinking fountain; these smartly dressed ladies have a drink of water from chained mugs.

Below: During the 1920s a diving platform was erected on Princess Pier which was used for swimming and diving competitions principally during Regatta Week.

DIVING STAGE, PRINCESS PIER, TORQUAY. 1927.

Above: Princess Gardens Promenade during the 1920s. The gardens were laid out in 1894 on three-and-a-half acres of reclaimed land and provided a fine attraction for both residents and visitors.

Below: The promenade between the pier and the Palm Court Hotel was widened during the period 1931 to 1934 and featured walled gardens.

On 23 April 1922 the war memorial was dedicated by the Bishop of Exeter and unveiled by Col. C.R. Burn, the local MP. At that time the memorial contained the names of 596 men who fell in the line of duty from 1914 to 1918.

Between the Pavilion Theatre and the pier was a landing stage used by ferry boats and other small craft. Adjacent was a tea garden strategically placed to catch the pleasure boat trippers.

The first reclamation prior to the laying out of Princess Gardens was a small area which covered over the beach in front of Cary Green and formed a short promenade towards the harbour. This work was carried out in the early 1870s.

A sheltered area protected from breezes lies to the harbour side of the Pavilion Theatre and provided another refreshment area.

The Pavilion Theatre was opened on 17 August 1912. During its construction special foundations were sunk deep into the reclaimed portion of Princess Gardens. Many famous artistes performed at the Pavilion during its use as a concert hall and theatre.

four

Harbour Area

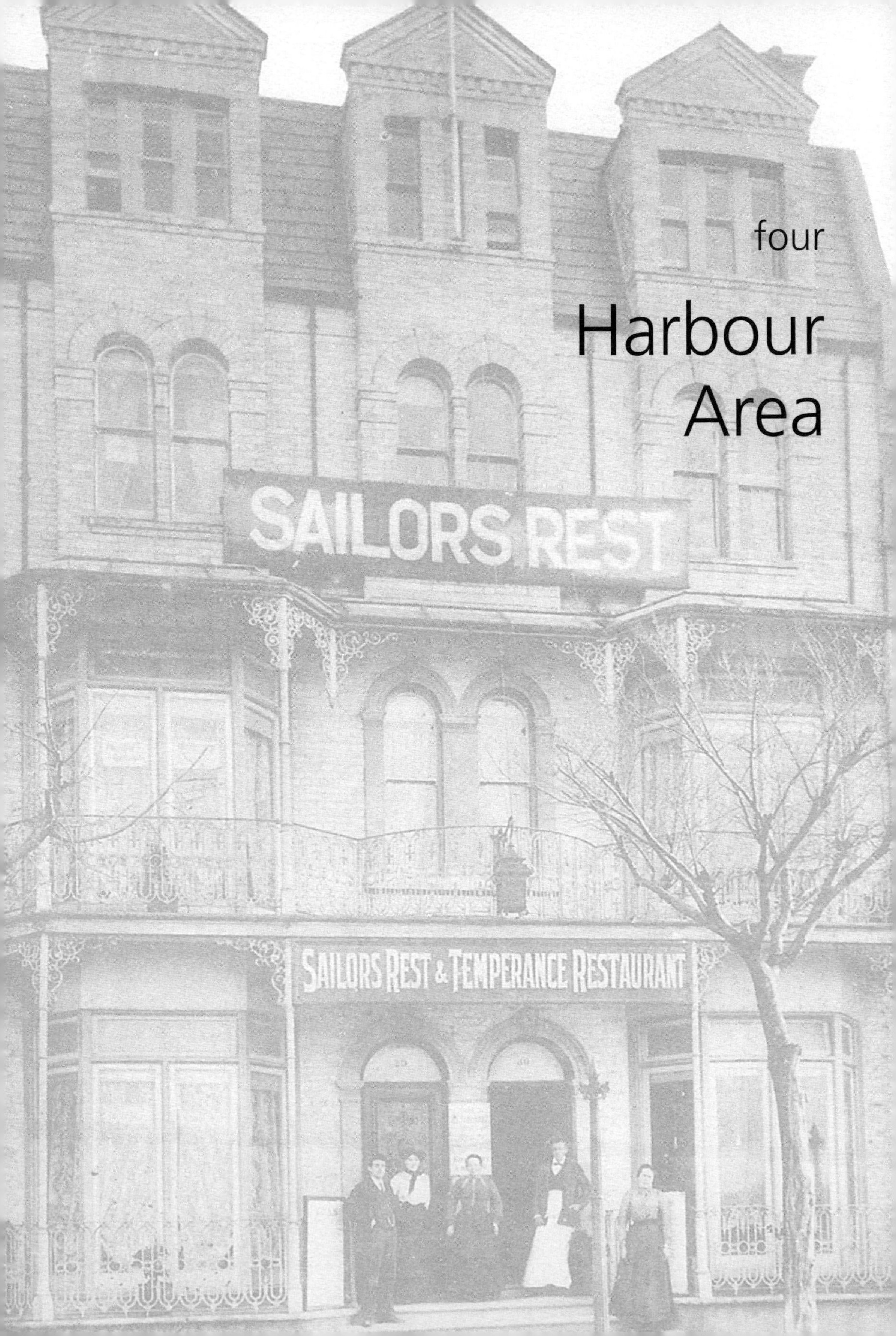

Torquay was fortunate in having for many years two major grocers. Both had been established in the 1830s and traded from excellent positions within a short distance of each other. One was Shapley's on the Strand and the other was Slade & Sons in Abbey Place. This is Slades' premises with a large group of employees assembled for the photograph. It includes members of the outside sales staff complete with sample cases ready to call on hotels and the gentry soliciting orders.

Opposite above: Cary Parade in the first decade of the last century when the houses on the left were still private residences. On the right is a hansom cab rank.

Opposite below: By the 1930s Cary Parade had changed and the first slot machine arcade had opened for business. The parade also included a gift shop and the well-remembered Addison's Café.

8502. CARY PARADE, TORQUAY.

In the early days of the last century it was still safe to walk across Abbey Place without fear of fast-moving traffic. On the left can be seen Lawrence Arch. On the right is the 'big tree' which was a feature of the area for about 100 years.

The 'big tree' features again in this image, *c.* 1905. The photographer is standing in the Strand looking towards Fleet Street. The blinds on the shops in the Strand are drawn to protect the merchandise in the shop windows from the sun's rays.

This engraving shows Abbey Place and the Strand in mid-Victorian times. The 'big tree' was even then a feature of the area. To the left can be seen Carroll's shop, which was a previous trading name for Shapley's.

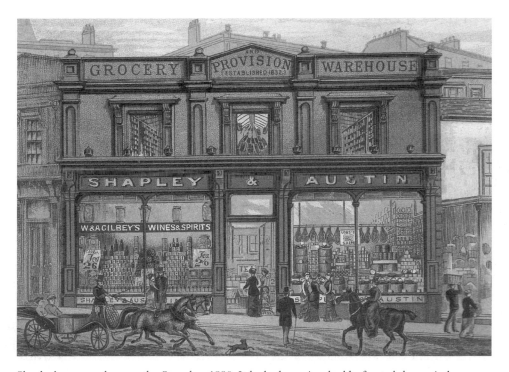

Shapley's grocers shop on the Strand, c. 1890. It had a large size double-fronted shop window. The aroma of coffee and other unwrapped foodstuffs would have enticed passers-by into this well stocked store.

Above: The Strand, *c.* 1890. The post by the kerb side is for attaching a shop blind. Slabs by the pavement were put there to allow gentlefolk to alight from their carriages without having to step into the dirty gutter.

Left: One of the major traders on the Strand for many years was Williams & Cox, with separate premises for their clothing, millinery and haberdashery shop and a few doors away the furnishing store. On 21 September 1939 the latter tragically caught fire, causing major damage within and to Bobby's premises next door.

On 12 August 1892 the Charter of Incorporation signed by Queen Victoria, which created Torquay as a Borough, arrived on the Strand to be greeted by local dignitaries and a huge crowd of rejoicing townsfolk.

This image from the 1840s shows a tree-lined Strand and Hearder's Family Hotel. Later it was renamed the Queen's Hotel and in the 1860s another storey was added. In the 1930s the hotel was rebuilt in the art deco style.

The Queen's Hotel with the hotel horse bus parked outside, *c.* 1910. It was for many years a popular hotel for those who preferred accommodation in the town.

Webb's Royal Hotel, which stood opposite the Queen's Hotel, is seen in this engraving from the mid-nineteenth century. It lost its position as the leading hotel once the Imperial Hotel opened and Thomas Webb moved from the Royal to the Imperial as manager.

Marchetti's Apsley House in what is now Meadfoot Road. In August 1845 the Dowager Queen Adelaide and her suite stayed for a few days, and in July 1854 Maria Amelia, a former Queen of France and her suite. Joseph Marchetti had previously been manager of the Queen's Hotel or Marchetti's Family Hotel as it was then known.

Torwood Street, *c.* 1905. On the right is the Rotunda, site of the old market originally established in 1820. By the early 1900s it was a retail branch of D.J. Allams & Son, china merchants.

One of the oldest established businesses in Torwood Street was Charles Heaviside, whose premises can be seen on the right. Previously trading as Reynolds Pianoforte Saloons it gave over 100 years service to the town by supplying sheet music, keyboard instruments and latterly wireless sets.

Holy Trinity church, erected in 1895. To the left is the former entrance to Torwood Gardens. Many years later the grounds at the end of the gardens were used to erect a large building which contained the Grey Cars Garage and Eric Perry, motor engineer. The pharmacy is still there trading as Quants.

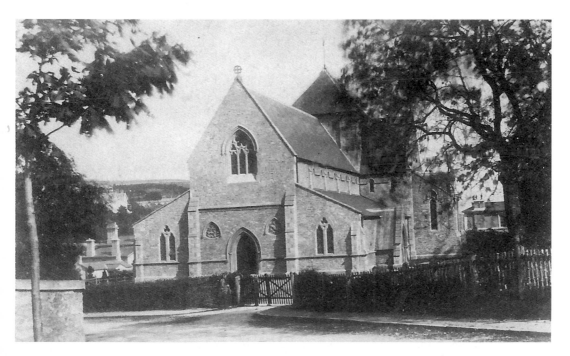

St Mark's church, designed by Anthony Salvin, was consecrated in October 1857. This photograph dates from the mid-1860s, just a few years after completion. It is now the home of the Little Theatre.

The Winter Gardens were erected on a site of four acres near Torquay Museum and partly opened in June 1881 at an estimated cost of £12,783. Constructed of glass and iron the building consisted of a winter garden with seating for 1,000 people, a restaurant, a billiard room, reading rooms, offices and an American-style bowling alley. Three tennis courts were provided. Unfortunately the venture lost money, and it was eventually sold for £1,300 and now occupies a site on Great Yarmouth seafront.

Right: The Sailors Rest at Nos 29-30 Victoria Parade was erected in the early 1900s and offered reasonably priced food and temperance accommodation to seafaring folk.

Below: The Fish Quay was once a busy place to see the morning's catch being unloaded and sold fresh on the quay to restaurant owners, hoteliers and individuals.

Big thrills were the merry-go-round and the helter-skelter and the annual visit of the fair was eagerly awaited by young and old.

Opposite above: Visits by naval ships were once a regular part of the summer life of Torquay. The sailors' trip ashore brought revenue to local traders and a smile to the faces of local girls. A naval launch is tying up ready to take crew members back to their ship, *c.* 1935.

Opposite below: Since the 1800s the visit of the funfair was always part of Torquay Regatta Week, with the amusements and rides assembled around the harbourside. Only in recent decades has the fair moved to Torre Abbey Meadow.

Torquay relied on shipping for the delivery to the inner harbour of raw materials for local consumption like coal and timber. Here we see a coaster being unloaded of its cargo of coal. This was at a time when most households had coal fires.

A shipment of timber has just been unloaded at Beacon Quay. Most of this would have been used in the building of new houses in the rapidly expanding areas of Shiphay and Chelston during the 1920s and '30s.

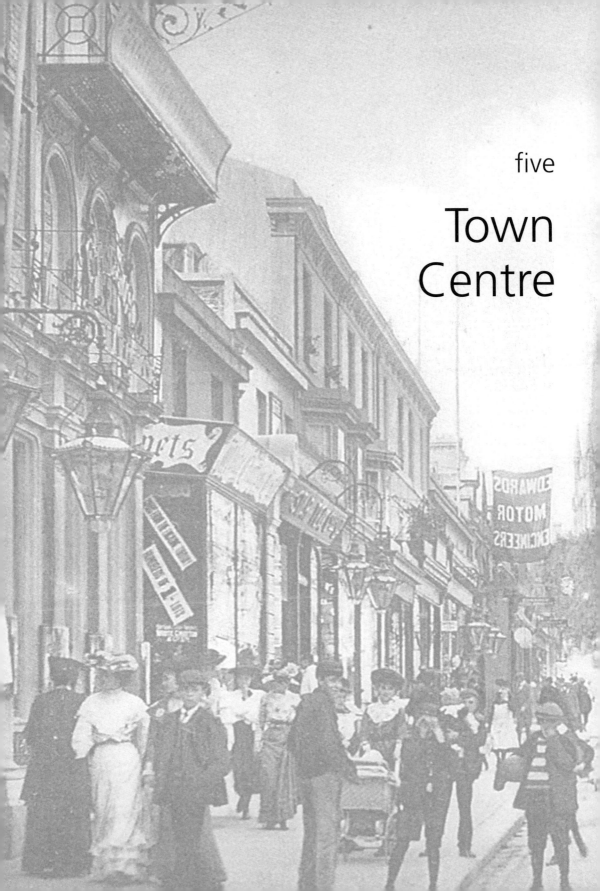

five

Town Centre

HOTEL ADYAR
Castle Circus :: Torquay

Left: Adyar Hotel in St Marychurch Road, overlooking Castle Circus, photographed at night during the 1930s. Previously known as the Rokeby Private Hotel, in more recent times it has become offices and meeting rooms for Upton Vale Baptist Church.

Below: On the other side of the road stands Glenthorne, which in the 1920s was a boarding house. For many years the premises have housed consulting rooms for the Terrace Dental Centre.

APARTMENTS
"GLENTHORNE"

Above: Work is underway preparing the site for the erection of the Regal Cinema in Castle Circus which opened in 1933. At that time Torquay already had two theatres and four cinemas playing to packed houses.

Below: The Regal had what in those days was a new attraction, a Compton organ which rose from beneath the stage to entertain patrons during the interval. For many years it was played by Reginald Porter-Brown.

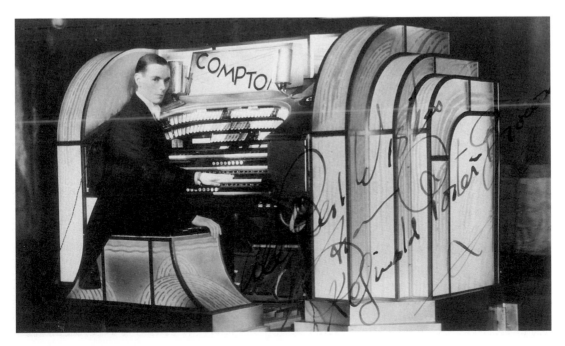

The Pavilion, a temperance, commercial and family hotel. Opened in the 1890s by the proprietor Mr W. Wood it advertised a restaurant, billiard room, hot and cold baths, and lavatories on all floors. It now consists of shops and offices.

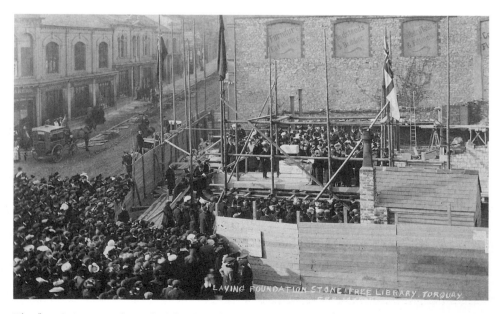

The foundation stone being laid for the Torquay Carnegie Free Library on 14 February 1906. The building was completed in 1907, financed from a beneficiary grant from the Andrew Carnegie Foundation.

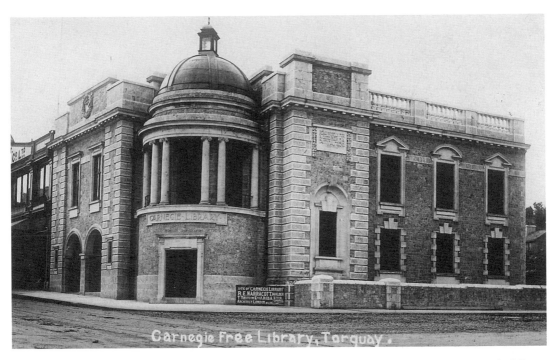

The Free Library was built by Mr R.E. Narracott, whose firm was responsible for many major building projects during the 1900s. The windows, doors and interior are awaiting attention. To the left is White, Chatton & Company Ltd, trading as 'The Exchange and Mart'. To the right can be seen the empty site where a new town hall would be erected a few years later.

In 1913 the town hall was completed in a style to blend in with the existing Carnegie Library building. When the new public library round the corner in Lymington Road was built the Carnegie library became the council's Borough Treasury offices.

The YMCA premises were opened on 31 May 1919. Mr White, when closing his business 'The Exchange and Mart', presented the premises to the YMCA (Young Men's Christian Association) in recognition of its valuable work for the country during the First World War.

The fire brigade, later the national fire service, used what is now the town hall car park as a training area. A 1930s fire engine with extension ladder is being given a thorough test. In the background is Upton Vale Baptist church. The small huts were used by charabanc operators as booking offices.

Above: Torquay Infirmary in Higher Union Street opened during the 1850s. For just over seventy years it was Torquay's main hospital and dispensary, and in the days long before the National Health Service was established it was supported by voluntary contributions, bequests and other donations.

Below: One of the male wards in Torquay Infirmary at Christmas, *c.* 1920. Without the benefit of modern drugs and nursing techniques the patients nevertheless received the best care and attention that was then available.

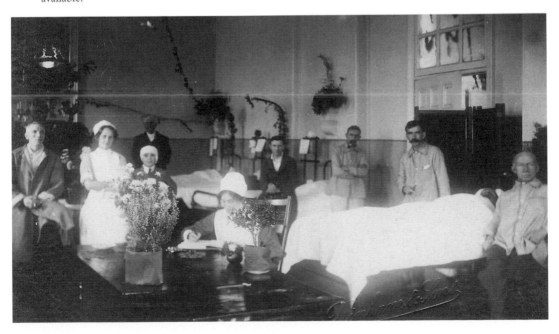

Above: In Union Street around 1905 horse-drawn transport still predominated. On the right is Union Street Methodist church. Shoppers in Edwardian dress throng the pavement, passing grocers, milliners, ironmongers, dairies and other traders now missing from modern shopping centres.

Below: A tram trundles up Market Street towards Ellacombe, *c.* 1910. A pedestrian walks in the road without needing to pay attention to fast moving traffic. People lived at a much slower pace a century ago.

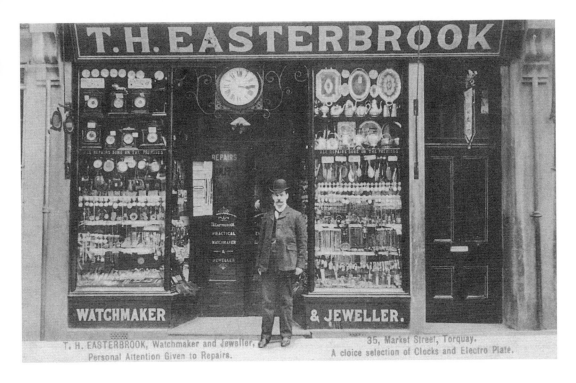

Above: Thomas Henry Easterbrook, watchmaker and jeweller, in around 1910 standing proudly outside his shop, which traded until well into the 1970s.

Right: The *Western Evening Herald* and *Western Daily Mercury* newspaper office in Union Street, next door to the old town hall early in the last century. Published in Plymouth, the office was used to accept advertisements and also sold a range of stationery and postcards.

Colonel Charles Rosdew Burn was the Conservative and Unionist candidate in the December 1910 parliamentary election, and successfully unseated Frederick Layland–Barratt by a narrow margin of 130 votes. Burn subsequently won two further elections in 1918 and 1922 and was the Torquay MP for thirteen years.

Francis Layland–Barratt unsuccessfully fought to be Torquay's MP on behalf of the Liberal Party in the 1895 parliamentary election. Subsequently he won the seat in 1900 and held it until the December 1910 election when he was beaten by Colonel Burn.

Above: The declaration of the result of the December 1910 parliamentary election attracted a very large crowd who assembled outside the old town hall to hear the results read by the returning officer. In January 1910 Layland–Barratt won by eleven votes and in December Burn was successful by 130 votes.

Right: Layland–Barratt stands to give his speech admitting defeat to his Conservative opponent. Apart from success in the 1923 election, which was short lived, the Liberals had to wait until recent years to once again send a successful candidate to the House of Parliament.

This picture shows the old town hall at the junction of Abbey Road and Union Street, *c.* 1865, indicating that the higher town had already taken the shape that we know today. The clock on the town hall reads ten past nine but there is not a person or vehicle in sight.

We move forward some forty years to capture this image of the town hall from Fleet Street. A tree has been planted by the junction of Abbey Road and Union Street. A steam-driven omnibus approaches *en route* to the harbourside.

The General Post Office in Fleet Street was opened in 1912. In those golden days there were up to six collections, and three deliveries of mail a day within the Torquay area.

J.F. Rockhey, the large building on the left, will be remembered by many as one of Torquay's finest department store. John Fry Rockhey was the mayor of Torquay from 1896-97 and again from 1901-02. The shops in the left foreground were all demolished in recent years to form the Fleet Walk development.

Fleet Street in the early 1900s. Note the juxtaposition of three eras of transport, the horse-driven carriage, the tramlines and the 1906 Hotchkiss open tourer motor car parked on the left. W.H. Smith & Son were well established on larger railway platforms and in the major shopping streets of major towns. Due to the Fleet Walk development it is now further up the road.

six

Marine Spa to Ilsham

During the late 1860s Beacon Hill was drastically reduced in size. The excavated limestone was used to build Haldon Pier and to transform the Bath Saloons into a larger Marine Spa. The railway line seen on the pier was used to transport the stone by wagon to the workmen involved in the strenuous work at the sea end of the pier. Work had just been completed on the additional wing of bedrooms at the Imperial Hotel, necessary only four years after opening. Extending out to sea from the Marine Spa are the remains of an old pier, long abandoned.

The Marine Spa was a popular rendezvous, where friendships were forged and locals and visitors learned to swim and to enjoy dances in the ballroom. By the 1930s the Vita Glass lounges were an added attraction for morning coffee and afternoon tea.

The interior of the Vita Glass lounge shows a typical 1930s café decor with glass-topped tables and comfortable wicker chairs looking out to wonderful sea views across Torbay.

An afternoon tea dance in the Marine Spa ballroom during the 1930s. On the left is the bandstand where popular combinations like the Blue Lagoon Dance Sextette played regularly for afternoon and evening dances.

Opposite above: Nestled beneath the Marine Spa was Beacon Cove. During the 1800s it had been the ladies only bathing beach but in later years became popular for families who were attracted by its sheltered aspect and good swimming and bathing facilities.

Opposite *below:* Tents were provided for bathers in Beacon Cove and the old lifeboat station was converted into a café for those who wished to have refreshments in pleasant surroundings.

Beacon Cove, Torquay.

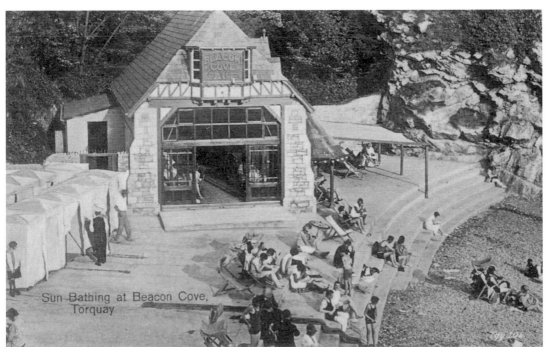

Sun Bathing at Beacon Cove,
Torquay

60 FT "SWALLOW DIVE
by F.J. COLLINGS. TORQUAY.

Left: F.J. (Tack) Collings was a very brave man. He could swallow dive 60ft from the top of Saddle Rock into 9ft of water. Tack had represented Great Britain in the 1908 London Olympic Games and later became a very accomplished trick diver. On behalf of Torquay Leander Swimming and Life Saving Society he taught many young people to dive but not from Saddle Rock. Present day 'tombstoners': do NOT attempt to copy – it is highly dangerous.

Below: Torquay Leander Swimming and Life Saving Society was formed during the last decade of the 1800s and soon became a popular club for local swimmers and divers. Preparations for the opening sea swim of the season in Peaked Tor Cove were captured on camera in May 1908.

Above: Daddy Hole Plain is today a popular place to park the car and gaze across the bay at the beautiful panorama. The same applied in the days of the horse-drawn carriage. These Edwardian families walk towards the safety rail to admire the lovely view.

Below: By the 1920s a beach café at Meadfoot Beach was already open for business. Bathing tents are in abundance replacing the old bathing cabins which had been there since the mid-1800s. The concrete promenade for beach huts was a later addition.

Soon after the end of the First World War Mr and Mrs Gegg opened the Ilsham Tea Gardens as a welcome break for ramblers and visitors to Kents Cavern. An accordionist entertains the patrons on a warm summer afternoon.

It is interesting to note that around 1930 camping was allowed in the meadow adjoining the Ilsham Tea Gardens. This was at a time between the two wars when hiking and camping were growing in popularity.

These houses in Ilsham Road, between the shopping parade and Kents Cavern, were built between the end of the 1800s and the early 1920s. A group of children pose patiently for the photographer in this 1905 image.

Ilsham Road shopping parade in 1905. Mainly small, privately operated businesses have served the local area from late in the nineteenth century and still continue to provide for the people of the village into the twenty-first century.

Above: The staff of Eastman's the butchers pose outside the Ilsham Road shop in this 1900 photograph. The small horse-drawn cart halted outside is possibly the delivery vehicle. Eastman's had several branches in the Torquay area and had taken over this business, previously operated by Mr A.H. Palk.

Opposite below: St Matthias' church at Wellswood was originally planned as a chapel of ease to the senior St Mark's church. Originally designed by Anthony Salvin, St Matthias' was later enlarged as it became inadequate for the size of the parish and St Mark's became the chapel of ease.

Right: For many years the Thomas family operated the tea house, the bathing cabins and the boating facilities at Ansteys Cove. Visitors would either arrive by boat from Babbacombe or Oddicombe or they would walk down the steep cliff path.

Below: A warm summer day and a party enjoy a relaxing few hours in Ansteys Cove. It is 1910 and it would be unseemly to show any bare flesh. The only way to get cool was to hire a bathing cabin, change into a heavy woollen costume and be wheeled down to the sea to enter the water and bathe.

The villa Bishopstowe, *c.* 1905. This was erected in 1841–42 for Henry Phillpotts who was Bishop of Exeter for nearly thirty-nine years. After Phillpotts' death the villa became the home of Mr and Mrs Sampson Hanbury and in 1906 it passed into the hands of Sir Arthur and Lady Elibank Havelock.

In 1920 Bishopstowe was purchased by a company who opened it as the Palace Hotel in August 1921. Although bomb damaged by enemy action during the Second World War the Palace Hotel survives as one of Torquay's finest hotels.

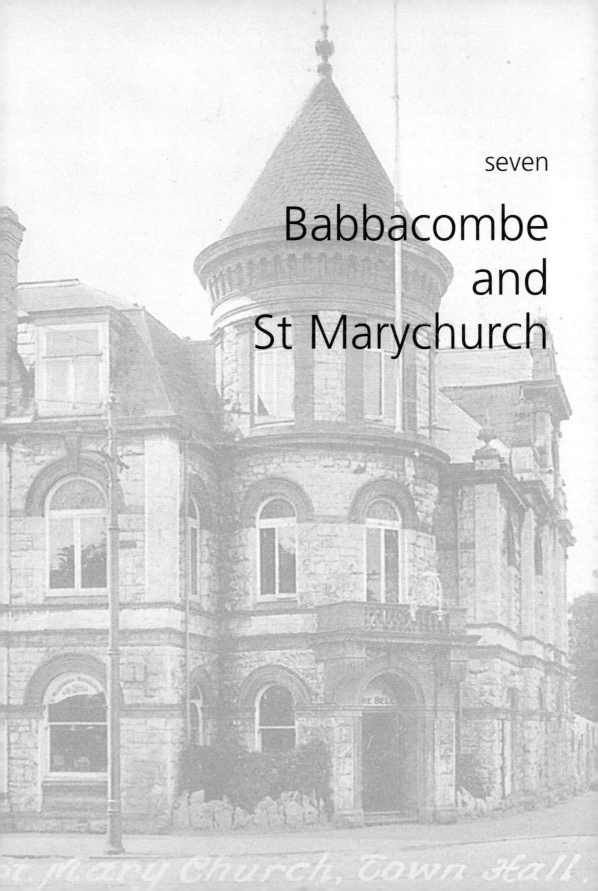

seven

Babbacombe and St Marychurch

ERECTED IN MEMORY OF R. S. S. CARY OF TORR ABBEY BY HIS WIDOW A.D.190..

Babbacombe lies on land which had been owned by the Cary family of Torre Abbey. Cary Park was gifted to the town by R.S.S. Cary in 1897 to celebrate Queen Victoria's Diamond Jubilee. This drinking fountain, now incomplete, was placed there in 1904 by Mr Cary's widow in memory of her late husband.

From a small fishing village Babbacombe grew in size, mainly during the latter half of the 1800s, as villas and terraces were built to house the ever-expanding population. This is Victoria Terrace in Babbacombe Road near the Masons Arms. St Anne's Hall can be seen in the distance.

Portland Road extends from Babbacombe Road to the Downs. In this photograph of around 1910 we note that the village policeman lived in one of the houses nearest the photographer.

Above: Reddenhill Road, *c.* 1910. Near the junction with Babbacombe Road people walk in the road without fear of fast-moving traffic. The village shopping parade is already open for business. In the foreground on the right Perinville Road is still only a grass track.

Looking every part the old salt, Richard Harris, complete with fisherman's jersey and telescope, poses outside his home, Beach Cottage. In 1906 sparks from a disastrous fire at the Cary Arms Inn ignited the thatched roof of the cottage causing severe damage.

Above: This photograph was taken some twenty years before the pier was constructed at Babbacombe beach in 1889. Two bathing cabins await customers. Note the amount of sand then present on the beach.

Opposite below: The building of York Terrace began in the 1860s. This scene was captured just over forty years later and a glimpse of a tramline can still be seen.

Lovers' Seat, Babbacombe Slopes, *c.* 1905. This was for many years a favourite spot for courting couples to dally for a while. This section of pathway is now closed to the public due to the danger of falling rocks.

Oddicombe Beach, *c.* 1905. The bathing cabins at Oddicombe then had a distinctive shaped roof and a few were still in use as late as the 1930s when they were replaced by bathing tents.

Oddicombe has long been a popular beach for swimming and bathing. The diving platform became a great attraction to youngsters during the 1930s.

The beach café at Oddicombe was a popular rendezvous from early in the 1900s. It began life as a single-storey building but an additional floor was added to meet extra demand after the cliff railway was opened in 1926.

PETITOR TEA BUNGALOW, PETITOR SLOPES, TORQUAY, 16396

CREAM
ICES
ICED DR
DECK CHAI

Petitor Tea Bungalow on Petitor Downs afforded lovely views of Babbacombe Bay. The bungalow was operated by Mr W. Tozer during the 1920s and '30s who advertised that it was just ten minutes walk from a tram stop.

St Marychurch town hall was built in 1883 to the design of G.S. Bridgman. It was used for meetings of the Urban District Council until St Marychurch and Babbacombe were incorporated into Torquay Borough in 1900. This image dates from around 1920.

Fore Street, St Marychurch, *c.* 1935. The Tudor Cinema can be seen on the right of this photograph. It has now become the popular 'Bygones' attraction. The land on that side of the road was once part of the Hampton House estate.

St Marychurch

Above: Fore Street again, this time looking down the older narrow part from near the parish church, *c.* 1905. This is now a popular pedestrian precinct.

Below: Looking up Fore Street from the other direction, *c.* 1905. On the left is Bendle's, a stationers and printers founded by Charles Bendle in the late 1800s. Next door is William John Waymouth, baker and confectioner.

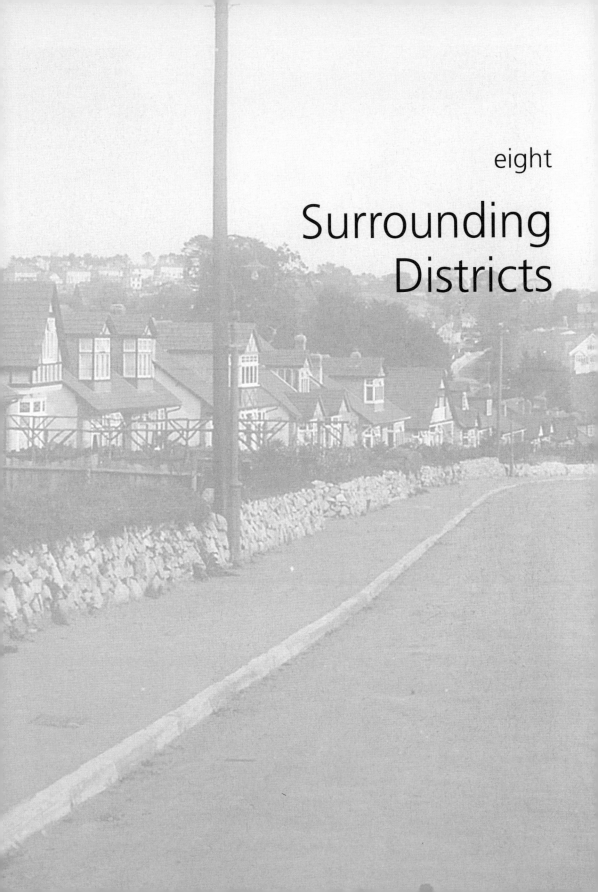

eight

Surrounding Districts

Belgrave Road was developed in the mid–nineteenth century to meet the increased demand for hotels and private residences in Torquay once the railway reached the town. Cash's and Atkinson's were the first two custom built hotels erected in the road in the 1860s but gradually the private residences were adapted into boarding house and hotels.

After Belgrave Road was built, further expansion followed with the addition of side roads. Bampfylde Road featured smaller terrace houses, many of which were used as boarding houses during the days of traditional family holidays in the 1900s.

Scarborough Terrace, linking Belgrave Road and Croft Road, *c.* 1910. On the other side of the road was Belgrave Crescent which looked out over the fine gardens of Croft Park, which later became the home of the Torquay Lawn Tennis and Croquet Club.

To serve the fast expanding community of Belgravia a shopping parade was established in Lucius Street. The businesses included a Shapley's branch shop.

To celebrate the Coronation of King George V and Queen Mary on 22 June 1911 a bonfire was built in Belgrave Road, next to the offices of Nicholson & Sons, on the corner of the tree-lined Bampfylde Road.

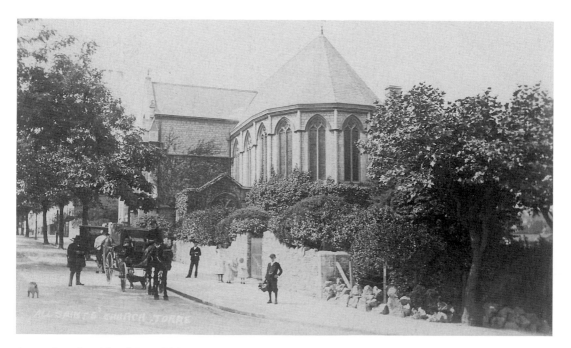

Across the other side of Bampfylde road is All Saints' church, which was erected in 1884 and replaced the temporary church which had stood there since 1867.

Taking part in pursuits which raised a bead of perspiration was not ladylike a century ago. These ladies are relaxing after a gentle game of croquet in the gardens of the Templestowe Hotel.

Chapel Hill was a popular place for a ramble and a picnic, with pleasant views from the top of the hill over the bay and surrounding countryside before the trees grew too tall and obscured the view.

Luxton's Upton Vale Hotel, Upton Road, c. 1920. It is possibly Mr Luxton standing outside. In recent years the property has been demolished to make way for a new development of residential flats.

St James' church, Upton. The foundation stone was laid in 1891 for what was then called St James Mission House. The bell turret was removed many years ago and the former church is now used by St James School and as a polling station at election time.

The oldest surviving memory of the old village of Upton is Penny's Cottage, which dates from the fifteenth or sixteenth century. Its present name stems from John and Peggy Penny who lived there until 1871. It is at the bottom of Penny's Hill, which is also named after them. Lying in ruins following a disastrous fire in 2005 work has now begun to restore it to its original appearance. In the background, on the top of the hill, is Daison Rock.

On 4 August 1938 Torquay was badly affected by flooding to the low-lying parts of the town. In particular Lymington Road, near the coach station, was flooded to a depth of about 2–3ft.

Ellacombe Green, where a match is in progress on the bowling rink, *c.* 1935. In the background is the Empire Cinema, opened around 1912 as 'The Cinedrome'. It later became a night club, but has since been demolished and residential flats now occupy the site.

Belmont Park, Ellacombe, just off Windsor Road, *c.* 1905. The neighbourhood youngsters are waiting to be photographed in the park, which was then fenced and featured a pathway.

Hoxton Road, Ellacombe, *c.* 1905. The grocer stands outside his shop, and the postman pauses on his round while the photograph is being taken. At this time there were six shops in Hoxton Road including a butcher's and a baker's.

Shiphay Collaton, *c.* 1925. Although Torquay was growing and expanding further into the countryside this part of the village still retained its rural atmosphere with thatched houses and some signs of farming activity.

Shiphay Collaton, *c.* 1925. The village post office and stores, then run by F. Wilson. In the background is St John's church, which was completed in 1897.

Shiphay Lane, *c. 1930*. The area saw rapid development during the 1930s, mainly in the vicinity of the Newton Road as the new hospital was built. John Lloyd the builders were advertising new modern labour-saving houses priced between £675 and £800.

Shiphay Collaton Farm, *c. 1910*. Many a tale is told of smuggling in the area in previous centuries. When this farm was demolished in the 1920s it was found to contain hiding places for contraband.

On 29 March 1930 His Royal Highness the Prince of Wales (later King Edward VIII) visited the new Torbay Hospital which had been opened in 1928. He spent his time at the hospital visiting several wards and departments. The signature on the postcard is that of Georgina Turner, the Matron, who accompanied the Prince during his visit.

The old hospital in Higher Union Street was by the 1920s too small for the needs of the expanding town and the decision was taken to build this new hospital at Shiphay. This was helped by a most generous gift from Mrs Ella Rowcroft of Pilmuir of £100,000 to help with purchasing the land and the construction of the new hospital

55288. The Children's Ward, Torbay Hospital, Torquay

The Children's Ward at the new hospital, also called the Louisa Cary Ward, c. 1930. One of the features of the ward was the specially commissioned wall tiles depicting popular nursery rhymes.

In the early 1900s Barton was a hamlet with the cottage homes of a few farmers and their labourers.

Barton, c. 1925. By this time a number of houses have been erected but the hamlet, fast becoming a village, still retained its rural atmosphere.

Barton, *c.* 1905. Looking down from the Quarry towards Dartmoor Cottage. To the right a pathway winds across the fields which are now covered by housing estates.

A tranquil scene of haymaking in the fields of Barton, *c.* 1910. In the days before mechanisation such work was labour intensive. The horse and wagon and farm labourers would work from dawn to dusk.

Opposite above: The Avenue, now Avenue Road, *c.* 1875. It was the carriage drive to the gates of Torre Abbey from the Newton Road and was fed along its length by Elm Avenue, Lime Avenue and Chestnut Avenue. This narrow section is thought to be near Torre Station.

Opposite below: The Avenue, again around 1865. Two ladies cross the road near the gates to Torre Abbey, adjacent to Chestnut Avenue and Lime Avenue. Although the buildings in Belgrave Road were under construction at this time the territory towards the Avenue and beyond was still of a rural nature.

Right: By 1910 the Avenue had become Avenue Road and had taken the shape we know today. The local postman stops for a leisurely chat and in the middle background is the Devon Rosery and Fruit Farm.

Below: From Shedden Hill we look out across the newly built area of Belgravia, *c.* 1870. In the distance can be seen the long line of trees along the Avenue which in due course would be felled and the road developed.

Old Mill Road, *c.* 1906. A boy pauses with his hoop to watch the photographer. A delivery horse and cart wait outside J. French the butcher's and the billboards outside the newsagents report the latest headlines.

Opposite above: Pomeroy Bridge and Sherwell Stream, Lower Chelston. Sharon House now stands nearby.

Opposite below: The stream in the last image now meanders through Sherwell Park. We are looking towards Mallock Road and Sherwell Lane in this image, taken around 1930 soon after the park was laid out.

Moving forward twenty-five years and in Old Mill Road horse-drawn traffic has given way to motor cars and motorcycles. In the middle distance stands Sharon House.

Old Mill Road and the Lower Chelston post office, then run by E. Chapman, *c.* 1920. A young girl stands by the gas lamp standard in this tree-lined parade of shops.

Walnut Road, Chelston, *c*. 1935. On the right can be seen the branch shop of Slade's the grocers which would have attracted custom from the Chelston and Cockington area.

A lady walks confidently in the middle of the road towards the shopping parade in Walnut Road, *c*. 1935. Although the gentry would have an account and have their purchases delivered, the average customer would shop as required and pay cash.

Other local titles published by Tempus

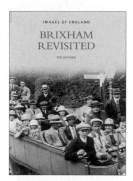

Brixham Revisited

TED GOSLING

This absorbing collection of images provides a nostalgic glimpse into the history of Brixham on the south Devon coast during the last century. Illustrated with over 200 postcards, this selection recalls Brixham in the heyday of its fishing past. From glimpses of shipbuilding, including the construction of the Mayflower II in 1957, to vistas of the old town streets and buildings, all aspects of working and social life are chronicled here.

0 7524 3620 1

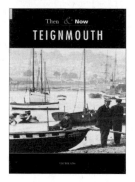

Teignmouth Then & Now

VIV WILSON

Teignmouth has seen many changes during its long history as a port, a fishing and boat-building town and a holiday resort. This book illustrates some of the changes that have occurred over the last hundred years by comparing a series of old photographs with modern ones taken from exactly the same locations. The reader can follow the changes and then revisit the locations to see them in a new light.

0 7524 3368 7

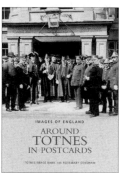

Around Totnes in Postcards

TOTNES IMAGE BANK AND ROSEMARY DENSHAM

This selection of 180 postcards from the Totnes Image Bank collection illustrates the bustling history of this town and the surrounding area, including Dartington, Ipplepen and Ashprington. The ancient castle and Elizabethan buildings are featured and events such as carnivals, Empire Day celebrations and the relocation of the Victoria Memorial Fountain are recalled. The images will evoke memories for some and provide a fascinating glimpse of the past for others.

0 7524 3190 0

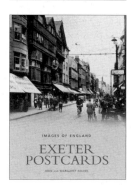

Exeter Postcards

JOHN AND MARGARET FOLKES

This is an exploration of Exeter and Exonians, in the dramatic first six decades of the twentieth century, seen through over 200 archive postcards. Subjects examined include momentous events such as the arrival of the first aeroplanes ever seen by Exonians and the many crises of accidents, fires, floods and war. Exeter Postcards provides a fascinating visual history of the city, which will surprise some and reawaken memories for others.

0 7524 3474 8

If you are interested in purchasing other books published by Tempus, or in case you have difficulty finding any Tempus books in your local bookshop, you can also place orders directly through our website

www.tempus-publishing.com